C000056672

HOW TO HAVE A CONVERSATION WITH GOD

Prayer That Draws Us Closer to the Father

HOW TO HAVE A CONVERSATION WITH GOD

DON M. AYCOCK

Kregel
Publications

How to Have a Conversation with God: Prayer That Draws Us Closer to the Father

© 2004 by Don M. Aycock

Published by Kregel Publications, a division of Kregel, Inc., P.O. Box 2607, Grand Rapids, MI 49501.

A revised, second edition of the previously published book *Be Still and Know,* © 1999 by Don M. Aycock.

Cover design: John M. Lucas

Library of Congress Cataloging-in-Publication Data
Aycock, Don M.
    How to have a conversation with God: prayer that draws us closer to the Father / by Don M. Aycock.
        p.   cm.
    1. Prayer—Christianity. I. Title.
BV210.3.A93   2004
248.3′2—dc22   2004000750

ISBN 0-8254-2002-4

Printed in the United States of America

04 05 06 07 08 / 5 4 3 2 1

How to Have
a Conversation
With God

Introduction

I have been interested in prayer all of my life. It's not that I am more "religious" than others. Often I think I am not particularly religious at all. Nor am I an expert on prayer. Instead, my interest in prayer grows out of a belief that we human beings are not alone on this planet. Ever since I was a child I have had an awareness that God is real and wants to have fellowship with us.

My modest hope for this small book is that you will grow in your knowledge that prayer is not a weird activity. It is a natural reaching beyond yourself, an exhaling that waits for the inhaling of the Spirit in order to be complete.

Take this little journey with me as we walk along and explore the country called prayer. Some of the landscape will be unfamiliar. Sometimes you may feel like you are in a foreign country. Relax. Let the place grow on you. Learn the language and customs.

Using the prayers I have provided here as a starting point for your own prayers, you will soon begin to develop your own prayer life. I hope you enjoy the time you spend with this book, learning how to have a conversation with God.

One day Jesus was praying in a certain place. When he finished, one of his disciples said to him, "Lord, teach us to pray, just as John taught his disciples."

—LUKE 11:1

*T*here is an ancient Roman word— *precarious*. It originally meant, "obtained by prayer or begging." Today something that is dependent on anything uncertain is called precarious. That is what some people think prayer is—a last resort, a beggar's choice, a weakling's fall-back. For all of the misunderstandings and even deliberate attacks on prayer, one fact is certain—people pray. They want some contact with truth, they want to know that life makes some sort of sense.

You are probably reading this book because you want to know this, too. Welcome. We will take this journey together. The trip will be worthwhile.

⁓

The "bottom line" for many of us regarding prayer is this: "Can prayer actually *do* something to make my life different and better?"

The answer is "Yes."

O God, teach me to pray. Help me to understand what reaching out to You means. This is a mysterious thing, but help me make it personal. Let me know You and learn to trust You.
In Christ, Amen.

*W*hat does the word *prayer* bring to your mind? A regular meeting at church? A last-ditch effort to stave off some disaster? An intimate communication between you and God?

All of these images, or others, might come to mind when we think of prayer.

❧

A ball game is about to begin. Silence is called for and someone begins to intone words of protection for the players. Is that prayer? A soldier in a battle raises his eyes to heaven in a silent plea for protection. Is that prayer? A woman kneels on a bench in a church building and begins to commune with God in a way that seems more like a dialogue than a monologue. Is that prayer? A young person faces an important test so she fingers the cross hanging around her neck. Is that prayer?

As is obvious by just these few images, prayer has many facets.

❧

George Appleton writes:

> The word "prayer" embraces a number of meanings and covers a number of activities. In its most elementary form it is asking God for the things we need, material or spiritual. It can be thanksgiving for what God has done for us; it can be worship of God for what he is. It can be fellowship with God, enjoying our touch with him, quiet reflection in his presence. It can be the expression of our concern for people or for what is happening in the world and in the church. It can be vocal, when we express ourselves in words, or it can be silent and contemplative, resting in his presence, the sphere of the timeless and the eternal. Prayer is as essential to the inner life as breath is to the body.[1]

Sometimes we can tell a lot about what a thing is by discovering what it is *not*. This is true with prayer. Consider some of the things prayer is not.

Prayer Is Not a Lottery

A lottery is a game of chance. A person gambles that what he bets will reward his efforts by paying off more than the original bet. It is very easy to think of prayer in this lottery fashion. We think, "Hey, I'll say a prayer in this situation. It couldn't hurt anything and it might pay off big."

But this way of thinking is purely selfish. The sole motive behind it is to gamble that a few words mumbled to a deity might "do some good."

Prayer Is Not a Twist of God's Arm

A popular notion about prayer is that it is a way to make God do something He does not want to do. It is a way to twist God's arm and force Him to do our will. Most of us would never state the case so boldly and probably many of us would even deny that is what we believe. However, when we listen to some of the things we pray for, and the way we ask for them, we realize that we are trying to force our will upon God.

Prayer Is Not an Automatic Guarantee of Success

A subtle, yet grave, misunderstanding of prayer is to think of it as merely a guarantee of success. Someone might think, "I really need to get an edge. I'll ask God to help me out."

We certainly want to pray in all things, but to imagine that prayer will give us a guarantee of success is immature. So how do we pray for things like our jobs and decisions we need to make? What good does prayer do in these situations?

Prayer Is Not Meaningless Ritual

My family has prayer at meal times. My wife and I have done this since we were first married and we have taught our children to say grace at the table. This ritual is important to us and it expresses our daily gratitude for our food. Many people say a prayer at meal times, or before bed, or at a ball game. The saying of the prayers might be meaningful or it might just be a ritual performed at stated times simply because we have always done it.

But prayer is not a meaningless ritual. It is far too important for that.

Prayer Is Not Getting in Touch with Mystical Powers

We live in an age of generic spirituality. We often hear about "spiritual values," but by that term many people mean inner personal values rather than a reference to God. A term that is often associated with spirituality today is *New Age.*

So what is prayer in New Age philosophy? It is the attempt to get in touch with the mystical forces of the universe and to influence those forces. That is done through repeating a mantra—a special word or phrase—or by deeply meditating. The attempt to influence the powers of the universe has traditionally been called magic.

Magic is defined as: "1. The art that purports to control or forecast natural events, effects, or forces by invoking the supernatural. 2. The practice of using charms, spells, or rituals to attempt to produce supernatural effects or to control events in nature."[2]

But prayer isn't "magic." It reaches out to the personal God, not to an impersonal force.

Lord, help me to understand.
Help me to offer my fledgling prayers
as best I can. When my words fail,
then know my heart.
In Christ, Amen.

C S. Lewis, a well-known writer from England, was especially careful not to allow prayer to sink to the level of seeming to be magic. He wrote, "The very question 'Does prayer work?' puts us in the wrong frame of mind from the outset. 'Work': as if it were magic, or a machine—something that functions automatically."[3]

His point is that prayer is communication between God and mankind, not a scientific formula in which everything is certain. Nor is prayer an "open sesame," guaranteed to open the doors of the universe to give you anything you want.

Prayer is not magic. It is more than that.

～

Prayer is different from magic and arm-twisting because it seeks to get in touch with, not a what, but a Whom. In other words, prayer reaches out to God as a loving heavenly Father who wants the best for His children rather than to a mysterious, capricious force of nature.

Prayer is personal communication that moves beyond the "gimme" aspect of life to communion with the Holy God. One person wrote, "The big watershed is moving from trying to control God to letting God direct me."[4]

You Are Invited to Pray

"Dear Friend, You are cordially invited to attend a meeting between you and God. The time is flexible, and you may accept this invitation as early as five minutes from now. Your Host is awaiting your reply. Please do not be long."

If this invitation arrived in your mailbox, how would you respond? My first response would be to check the postmark! Imagine it—an invitation from God Himself.

The whole concept of prayer is based on this one fact: *God wants to have communication with us.* That overriding fact needs to be kept in mind as we think about prayer.

To pray is to risk. The acclaimed author of *Roots,* Alex Haley, once said about taking risks, "Nothing is more important. Too often we are taught how *not* to take risks. When we are children in school, for example, we are told to respect our heroes, our founders, the great people of the past. We are directed to their portraits hanging on walls and in hallways and reproduced in textbooks. What we are not told is that these leaders, who look so serene and secure in those portraits, were in fact rule-*breakers*. They were risk-takers in the best sense of the word; they dared to be different."[5]

Be a risk-taker. Learn to pray.

❧

This is the beginning point of genuine prayer—a desire to reach out to God. The real quest of prayer is to know God, and not to get stuff. How different this is from the "name-it-and-claim-it" mentality that sees religious faith as a fast lane to riches! Prayer is interpersonal communication between a person and God. All of the open intimacy implied in communication is present. This includes everything from humor to anger, from request to praise. In prayer we can talk to God as we address another person.

For example, when I was a child, I used to tell God jokes. (Then someone spoiled this for me and pointed out that He already knew the punch line.)

❧

Why spend our time and energy in such an effort? What is the purpose of prayer? Donald

Bloesch, a theologian, has answered this question succinctly. He wrote,

> The ultimate goal of the life of prayer is the glorification of God and the advancement of his kingdom. Indeed, kingdom service is precisely what gives glory to God. To pray that the glory of God might be made manifest among people in the world is to pray for the fulfillment of God's highest will. It means to pray for the dawning of a new age, when all people may come to know the reality and sovereignty of God (Isa. 66:18; Phil. 2:10–11; 1 Peter 4:11).[6]

Our prayers are part of the means of having God's rule spread throughout the world.

So I say to you: Ask and it will be given to you; seek and you will find; knock and the door will be opened to you. For everyone who asks receives; he who seeks finds; and to him who knocks, the door will be opened.

—LUKE 11:9–10

The point Jesus was making had to do with His teaching on prayer. If an ordinary man can be moved by persistence, then Almighty God can be moved by it also. One person has said, "We must not play at prayer, but must show persistence if we do not receive the answer immediately. It is not that God is unwilling and must be pressed into answering," but rather, "if we do not want what we are asking for enough to be persistent, we do not want it very much. It is not such tepid prayer that is answered."[7]

When we pray persistently we accept God's invitation to a lifestyle of prayer.

Without persistence we would live as those who Theodore Roosevelt describes as being "in the gray twilight that knows not victory or defeat."[8]

The words "ask," "seek," and "knock" in the original language of the New Testament are present imperatives. A present imperative is a command to continuous action. Jesus thus said to the disciples, "Keep on asking; keep on seeking; keep on knocking."[9]

One quick prayer ripped off in a moment of need may or may not be answered. Jesus' point is that we can be assured of God's answer as we continue to seek God's will.

Some answers come only after much effort and patience.

God desires that we be hungry to learn from Him and to know Him personally. This takes both time and effort. He invites us to pray, but He will not make us pray. When we are hungry to know Him, we will find Him.

O God, help me to ask, seek, and knock. Help me to keep on asking and seeking and knocking, even when nothing seems to be happening. Accept the motivation I have, even if it is small, and help it to grow and blossom. Through Christ, Amen.

If you then, though you are evil,
know how to give good gifts to your
children, how much more will your Father
in heaven give the Holy Spirit to those
who ask him!

—LUKE 11:13

*P*eople who develop a life-long habit of prayer find that they move closer and closer to what God intends for them. They seek not their own wills, but God's will. They ask not for merely selfish goals, but for God's goals. They knock in order to receive what is best for them in the long run, not the short term.

One commentator has noted, "God does not have to be waked or cajoled into giving us what we need—many gifts he bestows on the ungodly and ungrateful; but his choicest blessings are reserved for those who will value them and who show their appreciation by asking until they receive."[10]

God's response to our prayers is consistent with His good nature. God loves people and wants the best for them. His gift of the Holy Spirit is evidence that God responds to prayer out of His goodness. Luke indicates that the Holy Spirit is the best gift God could give His children. Christians receive this gift at the time of their salvation.

Medical doctor and researcher Herbert Benson says that "humans are, in a profound physical way, 'wired for God.'"[11] He notes that we come into the world with hard-wired instincts such as fear of heights and fear of snakes. There are generally predisposed patterns of behavior.

He writes, "The idea that humans are wired for God, that we are custom-made to engage in and exercise beliefs, and that spiritual beliefs are the most powerful of that sort, felt like a truth that had always existed inside of me and inside of humankind to which I had suddenly gained conscious access."[12]

Our physically-based need to interact with God is powerful. Benson writes, "Religious groups encourage all kinds of health-affirming activities, fellowship and socializing perhaps first among them, but also prayer, volunteerism, familiar rituals, and music. Prayer, in particular, appears to be therapeutic, the specifics of which science will continue to explore."[13]

Benson has come upon a scientific way of affirming what the Bible has already said in many different ways.

We have a need to reach out to God. Why? Because He has already reached out to us. That may be the physically-based situation that Herbert Benson calls being "wired for God."

Blaise Pascal, the seventeenth-century mathematician and philosopher, wrote this about faith: "The heart has its reasons, which reason does not know. We feel it in a thousand things."[14]

We may not be able to give an adequate explanation for our urges to pray, but our "heart has its reasons." We *feel* it is the right thing to do. That feeling, that urge to reach out beyond ourselves, is God-given. We might call it a "homing instinct."

Be careful not to do your "acts of righteousness" before men, to be seen by them. If you do, you will have no reward from your Father in heaven.

—MATTHEW 6:1

Prayer, like most acts, is best done for the benefit of God and His reign—not just people. Our prayers are not to be said just so other people will hear us pray and think, "Gee, that person certainly is religious." Prayer is deep personal communication between you and God. When it becomes a show or performance, it ceases to be prayer.

Jesus warned against publicity hunting—doing religiously showy things for people to see. When we do something for show, the praise we get from other people is the entire reward. There is nothing else. God considers the praises "paid in full."

Lord, I want to pray with correct motives. I need so many things. My family, work, and community all concern me. But mostly, Lord, I need You. Help me learn not only facts about prayer, but the joy of speaking with You. Through Christ, Amen.

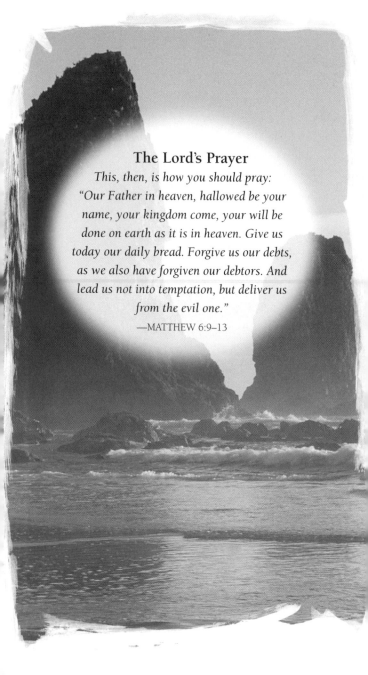

The Lord's Prayer

This, then, is how you should pray:
"Our Father in heaven, hallowed be your
name, your kingdom come, your will be
done on earth as it is in heaven. Give us
today our daily bread. Forgive us our debts,
as we also have forgiven our debtors. And
lead us not into temptation, but deliver us
from the evil one."
—MATTHEW 6:9–13

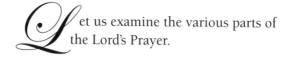et us examine the various parts of the Lord's Prayer.

"Our Father"

Jesus spoke in Aramaic, a language similar to Hebrew. He spoke of God as *Abba,* which is a personal term similar to our term "Daddy." This term expresses our relationship to God and His nature. God is not only the eternal Lord of the universe, He is also the Father of Jesus and of His followers.

This is a personal term of address. We may reach out to God with the realization that He is our heavenly Father who cares for us.

"In heaven"

While the term "Father" suggests that God is close and personal, the term "in heaven" reminds us that God is not just a good buddy next door. He is above and beyond us. God is not earthbound or temporary. He is heavenly and everlasting. He is transcendent.

God is bigger than all our ideas about Him.

"Hallowed be your name"

This part of Jesus' model prayer teaches us that God's name is separate from all other names. It is holy, which is the meaning of the word *hallowed.* In the Bible someone's name referred to his whole character. God's name is hallowed when His nature and purpose are known and reverenced. We should show reverence for God in our prayers.

"Your kingdom come"

God's kingdom is His rule in the hearts and lives of His people. To pray this part of the prayer is to pledge ourselves to join God's effort to extend His rule to everyone. This prayer is sincere when we want others to know the Lordship of God.

"Your will be done on earth as it is in heaven"

This is a request that God's purpose be carried out among persons. What is His purpose? Fisher Humphreys has written, "God's purpose is to create a worldwide family of persons who freely accept God as their God and who receive his love into their lives, and who respond to him by loving him with all their hearts and loving their neighbors as themselves."[15]

This, in a very succinct manner, is what God wills. When we pray "Your will be done," we are saying, "Lord, I want what You will for me. I pledge to work for Your purpose in life."

"Give us today our daily bread"

God's care for His children includes their total welfare. The needs of our bodies are important, as are the needs of our souls. Jesus taught that God is interested in our everyday needs. This includes food, certainly, but I think it includes all of our basic needs.

We may properly pray for *all* matters in our daily lives. This could include our home, our job, our health, our relationships with other people, and our deepest physical and emotional needs. Jesus taught that we can pray about everything that makes up daily life. We're invited to pray regarding our hurts, our hang-ups, our sexual desires, our loneliness, and anything else we may wish to share with Him and have Him assist us with.

In short, we may rightly pray about everything that touches our lives.

⌇

C. S. Lewis pondered the mystery of Jesus' teaching people to pray like this. Lewis wrote:

> Petitionary prayer is . . . both allowed and commanded to us: 'Give us our daily bread.' And no doubt it raises a theoretical problem. Can we

believe that God ever really modifies His action in response to the suggestions of men? For infinite wisdom does not need telling what is best, and infinite goodness needs no urging to do it. But neither does God need any of those things that are done by his finite agents, whether living or inanimate. He could, if He chose, repair our bodies miraculously without food; or give us food without the aid of farmers, bakers, or butchers; or knowledge without the aid of learned men; or convert the heathen without missionaries. Instead, He allows soils and weather and animals and the muscles, minds, and wills of men to cooperate with His will.[16]

By God's grace, our prayers matter to Him! Things happen when people pray. "God," said Pascal, a seventeenth-century philosopher, "instituted prayer in order to lend to His creatures the dignity of causality."[17]

Our prayers matter.

"Forgive us our debts, as we also have forgiven our debtors"

Forgiveness opens the door to relationships, both with God and with other people. Forgiveness is a spiritual nourishment that renews the mind and spirit the way food renews the body.

It is a two-way street that carries the traffic of incoming hurt and outgoing pain. Individuals can and should reach out to others and invite them to come close. Forgiveness is thus an open door through which we invite other people to be our companions. Without it, those doors remained sealed tight.

"And lead us not into temptation, but deliver us from the evil one"

This part of Jesus' prayer has troubled many people. Does God actually tempt us? The word "temptation" in the original language is *peirasmos.* It can mean both "temptation" and "trial." God does not "tempt" people with evil enticement. James 1:13 says, "When tempted, no one should say, 'God is tempting me.' For God cannot be tempted by evil, nor does he tempt anyone."

I think that Jesus meant that we should pray about the *trials* that come into our lives. One commentator says that the phrase "lead us not into temptation" means "do not let us fall into a trial so difficult that we will fail."[18]

This is a prayer for strength and help.

> *Thank You, Lord, for this model prayer. Help me meditate deeply on it and call out to You from its message. You are my Father; I honor Your name. I work for Your kingdom and I accept Your will. Thank You for my daily provisions. Help me forgive as I have been forgiven, and help me when I'm about to fall. In Christ's name, Amen.*

*Then Jesus told his disciples
a parable to show them that they should
always pray and not give up.*

—LUKE 18:1

Anyone who has been a Christian for very long and has done much praying knows that discouragement can often set in. We lift our voices to God but seemingly get nothing but silence. Jesus knew that this was the case, so He taught the disciples to pray in such a manner that they would not be discouraged by delays. The delays in the answer did not mean that God had not heard.

Jesus told the disciples that they must never give up as they prayed and worked. We can overcome possible discouragement by continuing to pray, no matter what.

⁓

Can anything lasting and worthwhile be gotten with little effort and in a short time? A career takes a long time to establish. A relationship takes time and effort to develop.

The same is true with prayer. The more we pray, the better able we are to pray. We become more comfortable with this way of expressing ourselves. We also become better able to hear God as He answers us. Even when the answer seems to be silence, we can endure it through persistence.

⁓

Just because events do not flow smoothly, does not mean that God is not in those events. The life of faith is a rough and rocky trail, not a six-lane super highway. Jesus said to pray your way through these difficulties and tough spots.

Samuel Johnson wrote:

> All the performances of human art, at which we look with praise or wonder, are instances of the resistless force of perseverance: it is by this that the quarry becomes the pyramid, and the distant countries are united with canals.
>
> If a man was to compare the effect of a single stroke of the pick-ax, or of one impression of the spade with the general design and last result, he would be overwhelmed by the sense of their disproportion; yet those petty operations incessantly continued, in time surmount the greatest difficulties, and mountains are leveled, and oceans bounded, by the slender force of human beings."[19]

Prayer done in faith and perseverance is among those strokes that level the mountain.

◈

John Bunyan said centuries ago, "Real prayer is a serious concern, for we are speaking to the Sovereign Lord of all the universe, who is willing to move heaven and earth in answer to sincere and reasonable prayer."

◈

Part of learning to pray is to humbly discover what Fisher Humphreys calls the three categories of prayer.[20]

First, there are some things God gives us whether we ask for it or not. He sends the sunshine and rain and oxygen to nourish our planet and us. We do not have to pray for those things. They are part of God's providence. Some things we get even if we do not ask.

Second, there are some things that we ask God for but He will not grant our request. He is wiser than we are. Some requests do not fit into His long-range plans for humanity. Other things we ask for might be harmful to us. Some things we do not get even if we ask.

Third, there are some things that come our

way only if we pray. This is the middle ground between the first and second category. For His own purposes, God chooses to grant some things in life only if we ask for those things in prayer.

So what should we ask for? Our ignorance and immaturity often confuses us. We may not know what to ask for. Humphreys suggests that we are driven back to ask for what we think is in keeping with God's will for mankind. "We ask, quite simply, for those things which we believe to be in keeping with God's purposes and thus to be best for ourselves and for those for whom we care: for food and peace for the world, for sensitivity to the needs of those around us, for a good education for our children, for strong and lasting friendships, for a vision of how we may serve God more productively, for healthy families, for guidance for those who must make decisions, for courage for the fearful, hope for the discouraged, wisdom for the confused, and health for the sick."[21]

We ask for what we believe is right. But we humbly admit that sometimes we do not know what is right. Even that can be a matter of prayer.

*O Lord, sometimes it's all
so confusing—this teaching and that advice.
Lord, help me remember the basic fact that I
am talking to You. I want to be honest and
open. Help me do that, no matter what.
Through Christ, who was honest
with You, Amen.*

*S*omehow just telling people that you are calling their name before God helps them. The late humorist, Lewis Grizzard, learned that fact late in his life. During a serious heart surgery, Grizzard developed complications that almost killed him. Speaking of those who cared for him while he was in the hospital, he wrote, "To a man and woman, those doctors and nurses said to me after the critical time had passed, 'We exhausted all medical possibilities. We did everything we knew to do for you, and it probably wouldn't have been enough. What saved you was prayer.'"[22]

⁂

Blaise Pascal, the seventeenth-century philosopher once wrote, "When I consider the short duration of my life, swallowed up in the eternity before and after, the little space which I fill and even can see, engulfed in the infinite immensity of spaces of which I am ignorant and which know me not, I am frightened and astonished at being here rather than there; for there is no reason why here rather than there, why now rather than then. Who has put me here? By whose order and direction have this place and time been allotted to me?"[23]

Pascal was astonished that he had been given

the gift of life at all. I am, too. What further astonishes me is that I have the ability to change my life and the lives of others.

So do you. That way is through prayer.

⁓

Henry David Thoreau wrote, "However mean your life is, meet it and live it; do not shun it and call it hard names. It is not so bad, as you are. It looks poorest when you are richest. The fault-finder will find faults even in paradise. Love your life, poor as it is. Humility, like darkness, reveals the heavenly lights. Superfluous wealth can only buy superfluities. Money is not required to buy any necessary of the soul."[24]

Thoreau was on to something important. Modest living helps us keep our eyes off ourselves and helps to keep the focus on God. Being focused on something outside of ourselves helps us see others as needy children, or potential children, of God. We can pray for them and lift them up.

⁓

Remember that praying is work. It is real, effort-filled toil. You struggle to pray and to keep praying even when you do not see instant results. Charles Rabon was correct when he wrote, "God has no microwave saints. They aren't made that easily or quickly."[25]

Jesus said, "Love your enemies and pray for those who persecute you" (Matt. 5:44b). Love your enemies—what a command that is! We might feel more like cursing them or ignoring them. Praying for them is probably the last thing on our minds. But the attitude of the Christian is no longer his own. As Paul put it in Philippians 2:5, "Your attitude should be the same as that of Christ Jesus."

Praying for his or her enemies distinguishes the Christian from everyone else. It is appropriate behavior for followers of Jesus.

During the final day of his earthly life Jesus was crucified on a cross. This was a tortuous death. If He would ever have gone back on His teaching, surely it would have been at that time. But look at what happened. Luke 23:34a says, "Jesus said, 'Father, forgive them, for they do not know what they are doing.'" He not only taught that we should pray for our enemies. He set the example Himself.

I heard of a letter that was found in a baking powder can hanging on the handle of an old pump. The pump offered the only drinking water on a long and seldom-used trail across the Amargosa Desert in Nevada. The letter read:

> This pump is all right as of June 1932. I put a new sucker washer into it and it ought to last five years. But the washer dries out and the pump has got to be primed. Under the white rock I buried a bottle of water, out of the sun and cork end up. There's enough water to prime the pump, but not if you drink some first. Pour about one fourth and let her soak the leather. Then pour in the rest medium fast and pump like crazy. You'll git water. The well has never run dry. Have faith. When you git watered up, fill the bottle and put it back like you found it for the next feller. (signed) Desert Pete.[26]

Praying for an enemy is a lot like that. It is an act of faith that "primes the pump" in relationships. It also gives something back for the coming generation because it helps break the cycle of hate and fear. It's *tough!* But it's necessary.

Lord, I have a really tough time praying for _____. You know why. You know what happened. The pain and shame are still real. On my own, I cannot do anything about it. But with You, I can. Lord, here and now, I pray for _____. As fully as I am able, I forgive. Teach me to let go of the pain and to accept Your forgiveness, cleansing, and love. Through Christ, who forgave His enemies and prayed for them, Amen.

"If God knew how I really felt,
I'm not sure what He would do."

$\mathscr{T}$hus began a conversation with a friend on the nature of God and the friend's doubts. We were not long into the conversation before I discovered that this friend felt like he was the only person having difficulty with faith. To his relief I showed him that others, even in the Bible, have had trouble with their religious commitments.

The prophet Jeremiah was one such person. For him faith was not an escape from reality. It was just the opposite—a movement toward the source of all truth and reality. That source is God.

My friend's comment shows several misconceptions about God. First, he thought that God did not know how he felt—"If God knew . . ." Second, he thought that if God did know, He would be angry and/or disappointed. Third, he felt that the road to faith and piety lay in hiding feelings and doubts rather than exposing them to the fresh air of Scripture, shared wisdom, and honest prayer.

In short, my friend, and probably countless others, wondered about this fundamental question of faith: "Can I be completely honest with God, and tell Him my doubts and complaints as well as my faith and strength?"

If we seriously read the Bible, we will learn quickly that God seldom gives simple, trite answers to our questions. Instead, He challenges us to grow and develop spiritually. He wanted Jeremiah to get stronger in his smaller trials so that when the larger ones came, he would be ready (see Jer. 12:1–5). Genuine prayer is no trivial pursuit.

Think back over the last two years. Have you encountered any trials which could be preparing you for things to come? Perhaps you felt overwhelmed already and hoped nothing worse would come along. Why not make this a matter of prayer? Speak openly to God about it. But remember, you may get an unexpected answer.

C. S. Lewis once said, "Prayer is either a sheer illusion or a personal contact between embryonic, incomplete persons (ourselves) and the utterly concrete Person."[27]

Prayer is radical honesty.

We sometimes hear well-meaning people say, "Just pray and everything will be all right." But not everything is all right. Loved ones die. We have financial struggles and setbacks. Personal relationships get fouled up.

The trouble with this simplistic thinking is that it is not biblical. Jeremiah knew that no amount of false piety would ever bring him to a deeper understanding of God's purposes in this world. Read Job 1–8 and Paul's letter to the Philippians. You will discover two men wrestling with things that have gone wrong, things not according to their plans. But you will also discover two men who were honest with God and who would not give up. Such was the case with Jeremiah (see Jer. 20:7–18). Like Jacob wrestling with the angel at Jabbok (Gen. 32:22–32), Jeremiah refused to give up until he was blessed.

Are you facing some tough times? Don't give up. Honestly pray about everything.

It really does make a difference.

A cartoon shows a pastor in his study. His is kneeling in prayer as the secretary comes in with a handful of papers. She looks down, sees the pastor praying and says, "Oh, good, you're not busy."

What do you make of this situation? Is he busy with something momentous and urgent, or is he just fiddling with some trifle until he has something better to do? I can answer that question from my own experience.

Without prayer, I'm as good as dead.

We human beings are weak and needy creatures. That is because we are so complex and
full of potential. Our very potential marks us
for temptation and weakness. Temptations are
downward pulls that touch us at important
points in our lives. We are seldom tempted with
something unimportant.

In all times of testing, temptation, and grief
we can seek spiritual strength through prayer.

Throughout the previous chapters on prayer
we have seen that prayer is not magic or a gim-
mick that allows us to get whatever we desire.
Prayer is our heart communicating with the
heart of God. It is our mind pouring itself out
to the mind of God. Prayer is essentially personal in that it takes all that we are and gives it
to God. Jesus shows us how to pray when we
need God's strength.

Prayer is sometimes a wrestling match of
the soul, a wrestling match with God. Jesus
told a parable about an unjust judge and a

persistent widow to teach that people should keep praying and searching and not to give up (Luke 18:1–8). This perseverance is often called importunity.

Curtis Mitchell has written, "Importunity is an instructor in God's school of Christian development. In short, God does not become more willing to answer because of perseverance, but the petitioner may become more capable of receiving the answer."[28]

The late British theologian P. T. Forsyth was on target when he wrote, "Lose the importunity of prayer, reduce it to soliloquy, or even colloquy, with God, lose the real conflict of will and will, lose the habit of wrestling and the hope of prevailing with God, make it mere walking with God in friendly talk; and precious as it is, yet you tend to lose the reality of prayer at last."[29]

Life's most important decisions require life's most important resources.

One of those is prayer.

Praying for spiritual strength is appropriate in times of grief and distress.

When death comes to loved ones, pray.

When temptations come, pray.

When plans are shattered, pray.

Prayer is personal communication between you and God. It is never out of place.

Praying to know God's will is one thing. Praying to *do* it is something else. Doing that will require faith and courage. We should pray to find God's strength in times of stress. But we should also commit ourselves to do God's will regardless of the outcome.

Going a little farther, he fell with his face to the ground and prayed, "My Father, if it is possible, may this cup be taken from me. Yet not as I will, but as you will."

—MATTHEW 26:39

I once tried to talk to a man about God. He told me that when he was young his grandmother with whom he lived became ill. He prayed that she would get well, but she died instead. He said, "If God is real and hears prayer, why didn't He answer me?" Anyone can pray but not everyone is prepared to accept God's answer. That man did not seem to realize that God had said "no" to his prayer.

Jesus' prayer in Gethsemane indicates that He knew the difference between calling on God to get our way and calling on Him to find His way. We may legitimately call upon the Lord for anything that concerns us. We should seek what God wants for us so we can do His will. This is not always easy but it is always important.

⟨divider⟩

Jesus said, "Watch and pray so that you will not fall into temptation. The spirit is willing, but the body is weak" (Matt. 26:41). Prayer keeps us on our guard against temptations to sin. Temptation itself is not sin. A temptation is a suggestion or an urge. We cannot always control these but Jesus warns us to be on our guard against following through with every urge and desire.

C. H. Spurgeon, a nineteenth-century British

preacher, used to say, "I cannot prevent the birds of temptation from flying over my head but I can prevent them from building a nest in my hair!"

⚮

"Get real!" a woman once told me when I was speaking about prayer. She continued, "Prayer is okay and it makes you feel good. But in the real world it doesn't make any difference. Does prayer really help when we face tough problems?" Her question is an important one.

Yes, prayer really helps us when temptations and trials come. Prayer is not a magic carpet that zips us away from the trouble. It is quiet communication that helps us realize we are not alone in our struggles.

⚮

Lord, You know the problems I face, and You know the temptation I face to ask You to make them all disappear. Help me to handle my difficulties with faith and prayer. Let me do my best. I trust You for your help. In Christ, Amen.

And being in anguish, he prayed more
earnestly, and his sweat was like drops of
blood falling to the ground.

—LUKE 22:44

*P*rayer has many beneficial effects. Dr. Herbert Benson, a professor at Harvard Medical School, has identified what he calls the "Faith Factor" in physical and emotional healing.

The "Faith Factor" is the natural healing process that is made possible by the interaction of two forces. The first is a strong personal belief system that accepts the importance of caring for the body. The second is the practice of prayer and meditation as a part of those beliefs.

Benson noticed that people who have firm religious or philosophical convictions and who practice meditative prayer have the most success in healing certain conditions. These include helping to reduce high blood pressure, ease headaches and backaches, and overcome mental depression.[30]

Dr. Kenneth Cooper, the doctor who brought the word *aerobics* into common use, noticed the same thing. Cooper reviewed Benson's work, and the research of others, and came away with these observations. "As a Christian and a physician, I find such research to be quite encouraging because I do believe that there is a continuum between natural and supernatural healing. It makes sense to me that deep faith, enhanced by a developed life of prayer and meditation, would have a positive influence on the way our God-given bodies function and heal."[31]

Prayer helps to heal the body and the spirit. It helps us know we are not just some fluke of nature or an orphan in the universe. Prayer is real, and so are its results.

Very little in the spiritual life is easy. Make no mistake about that. Life in the Spirit is often difficult (but, of course, life in general is difficult).

Jesus Himself prayed three different times in His struggle to do God's will. Consider Luke's account of this night. He wrote, "And being in anguish, he prayed more earnestly, and his sweat was like drops of blood falling to the ground" (22:44).

What are we to make of Jesus' prayer? Why would Jesus pray like that? Read the entire story in the New Testament and you will discover that Jesus was a real man. Yes, He was unique— the very Son of God. But He was flesh and blood, too.

The early church referred to Jesus as "fully

man, fully God." He *struggled* in the garden of Gethsemane about His destiny. The battle going on in His mind was not a sham fight. He wrestled with all the normal human emotions and desires that others have, but He also fought to keep focused on the most important thing, namely, what God willed. Prayer helped Jesus to affirm His mission and see it through.

❧

Jesus faced His most trying hour in Gethsemane. His prayers strengthened Him to face that time. Our greatest challenges can be met with similar resources.

❧

Praying for spiritual strength to do God's will should include a commitment to do it, no matter what. Jesus was committed to carry out God's will regardless of what it brought. If you pray to discover God's will, be prepared to do it. Otherwise, why bother?

What is the one most challenging issue facing you right now? Design a prayer strategy to deal with this challenge.

O Lord, You have brought me this far. Help me now keep learning, keep trusting, keep praying. Give me strength and direction for the journey. Through Christ, Amen.

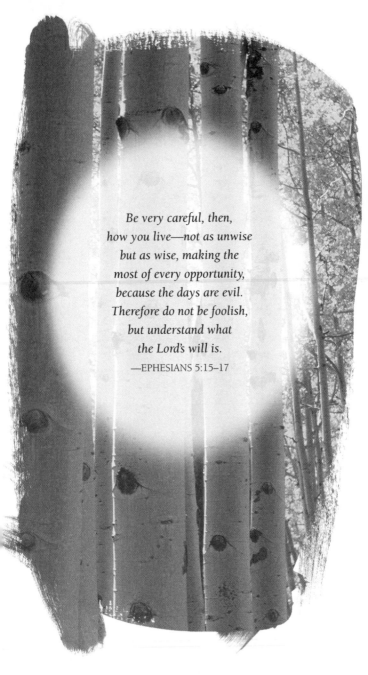

*Be very careful, then,
how you live—not as unwise
but as wise, making the
most of every opportunity,
because the days are evil.
Therefore do not be foolish,
but understand what
the Lord's will is.*
—EPHESIANS 5:15–17

*A*sk yourself a simple question: Where does prayer fit in with God's will for my life? To help answer this question, let us briefly explore the general nature of God's will.

There is much confusion about the concept of God's will. Some people think of God's will as being a target with a bull's-eye. The key, they think, is to fire at the target and hit the center every time. Any shot outside the bull's-eye is thus a shot outside of God's perfect will. But is that really an accurate image of God's will? I do not believe it is.

⚜

Let us reexamine some of the phrases that are often used in connection with God's will, phrases such as "God showed me," "discern the Lord's mind," "the very center of His will," and so on.

Theologian Gary Friesen makes a strong statement about these and other like phrases. He writes, "Such terminology reflects the conviction that the key to making the 'right' decision is discernment of God's ideal plan. What is so striking, as one searches the pages of the New Testament, is the *glaring absence* of such expressions."[32]

Friesen points out that the New Testament does not approach the will of God with the metaphor of an arrow hitting a bull's-eye. Instead, it pictures Christians who use their minds to perceive what God has revealed for all people. His argument flows as follows:

> In the progress of His revelation, God moved from a highly structured system of regulations governing a wide range of specific behaviors to a system where behavior is to be determined by principles and governed by personal relationship. There was a progress from law to Christ, from the bondage of close, restrictive supervision appropriate to immature and willful children to the freedom of responsible adulthood.[33]

I think God intends His children to grow up and use their wisdom to discover what God wants them to do. Many people approach the idea of God's will as if they think that all people remain infants who need to be taken by the hand and walked all the way through life. The Scriptures call us to grow up in our faith and to use our God-given wisdom to live a wholesome, well-rounded life in relationship to God and to other people.

~

Does God have a minutely detailed plan for every person? Friesen says, "If God's plan is thought of as a blueprint or 'dot' in the 'center of God's will' that must be discovered by the decision maker, the answer is no. On the other hand, we affirm that God does have a plan for our lives—a plan that is described in the Bible in terms that we can fully understand and apply."[34]

I agree. On the whole, the Bible does not give us a prescription for finding the "center of God's will." What it does do is call us into relationship with God through Christ and then challenges us to live according to what He has *already* revealed.

~

Think about it this way. The late English theologian John Oman said that God does not do His work like an archer firing his arrows straight into a target. Instead, God works the way rain falls onto the mountains and then finds its way down into streams and through rivers into the oceans.

The water ultimately reaches the ocean, but the trip could have been made by many routes.

To apply that analogy to our lives, when we give ourselves to God through faith and prayer, God's will is ultimately achieved. But in the meantime He allows human beings to participate in its accomplishment.[35]

The traditional approach to thinking about God's will is almost a needle-in-a-haystack approach. The sheer number of factors that could be involved is mind-boggling. Take the issue of finding a mate, for example. Some people say that God has one person already prepared for everyone—a "Mr. Right" or a "Miss Right." But the logistics of finding that one person out of so many possibilities is overwhelming. If a person does not find that one perfect mate, does that mean he or she has sinned and is out of God's will by marrying someone else?

I do not think so.

Instead of only one person being a potential mate, there may be many. To find God's will in the matter is to take seriously what the revealed will of God—the Bible—teaches us about Christian marriage. For example, we are not to be yoked with an unbeliever (2 Cor. 6:14); we are to have mutual respect for our mate (Eph. 5:21–33), and so on. More than one person will fit these criteria. Our job is to make mature, thoughtful decisions about the matter.

Do I love and respect this person? Does he or she have the personal qualities that I admire? Do I want to spend my life with that person? Prayer in these types of matters helps to clarify our thoughts and to center us on what is really important.

*O Lord, help me make
wise decisions. Help me use all of
the intelligence and insight You have given
me. I bring before You all of the important
people, events, and situations in my life.
Help me know how to deal with them.*

*Lord, I accept the fact that I have
to make my own decisions. I accept the
responsibility for those choices and I
refuse to blame anyone else. With
Your help, I'll do my best.
In Christ's name,
Amen.*

*N*o one, not even God, will make your decisions for you. God expects us to grow up in our faith, to make wise, mature decisions about all areas of life. J. I. Packer defines wisdom this way: "Wisdom is the power to see, and the inclination to choose, the best and the highest goal, together with the surest means of attaining it."[36]

Gaining this wisdom takes humility, work, and patience. The characteristics of biblical wisdom include reverence, humility, teachableness, diligence, uprightness, and faith.

Prayer helps pull all this together for us.

Prayer requires wisdom.

Gary Friesen writes about this wisdom as follows:

> The Christian *attitude* is to reflect, first of all, his awareness that no man, himself included, is naturally wise in himself (Proverbs 3:7); and therefore, if he is to gain wisdom, it must come from some other source. Equally, his attitude must mirror his conviction that the ultimate source of wisdom is God alone. Those who

refuse to acknowledge these basic realities are self-deceived fools (Romans 1:21–22). But the posture of the one who would find wisdom is that of bowing.[37]

Wisdom is necessary to make good decisions in life. Humility is necessary to gain wisdom. Prayer is necessary to gain humility and wisdom.

Prayer is thus essential to making good decisions in the issues that affect our lives.

Finding the will of God is not nearly as difficult as some people claim. God has a general will for everyone. Paul wrote to the Ephesian Christians, "Therefore do not be foolish, but understand what the Lord's will is" (Eph. 5:17). Earlier he had said to them, "For I have not hesitated to proclaim to you the whole will of God" (Acts 20:27).

How did Paul know "the whole will of God" for the Ephesians? He knew because God's general will for them is the same as for everyone else. For example, "The Lord is not slow in keeping his promise, as some understand slowness. He is patient with you, not wanting anyone to perish, but everyone to come to repentance"

(2 Pet. 3:9). To young Timothy, Paul wrote, "This is good, and pleases God our Savior, who wants all men to be saved and to come to a knowledge of the truth" (1 Tim. 2:3–4).

That, on the whole, is what God wants.

❧

God wants people to be saved. Salvation comes about when people give themselves completely to God and allow Him to transform them into the likeness of Christ. We learn about that desire from the Bible and from the lives of other Christians. We should be very careful about other purely subjective means of knowing something about God and His will. One scholar wrote, "Christians . . . do not behold a pillar of fire for assurance of God's presence. . . . Instead, they rely on the Word of God for both."[38]

❧

So God desires salvation for all people. We participate in that salvation when we accept it as God's gift, and as we pray that others might become open to it also. As we "grow up" in our faith and prayer life, we become less self-oriented and more God-oriented.

Fisher Humphreys said of this orientation

toward God, "Because he loves us, he will hear when we speak to him on any topic we care about. But precisely because he loves us so much, he wants us to become concerned about his 'adult' purpose. Ideally, our prayer should more and more be about achieving his purpose. We ought to be talking to him about the community, about its growth in faith and love, about the freedom of mankind, about the proclamation of the good news about Jesus."[39]

⁂

When we pray for God's will it is "not an attempt to second guess God, asking for what God was going to do anyway. It is rather talking to God about achieving his purpose, and asking him to do those things which we believe will carry forward his purpose."[40]

What this means is that we will not always get our way. Prayer is not a tool for prying out of God what He is unwilling to give.

⁂

On the occasion of his eightieth birthday, John Quincy Adams said, "John Quincy Adams is well. The house in which he lives at present is dilapidated. It is tottering upon its foundation. Time and the seasons have nearly destroyed it. Its roof is pretty well worn out. Its walls are much shattered and it trembles with every wind. I think John Quincy Adams will have to move out of it soon. But he himself is well, quite well."

That is what God wants for us, too. He is willing to give us fullness in our spiritual lives (John 10:10), and a sense of wholeness despite our circumstances.

Lord, I believe You want the best for me. I sometimes get tired and discouraged. But help me remember that You offer abundant life and strength every day. Thank You for all You do for me. Help me to keep trusting You. Through Christ, Amen.

A spirit of wholeness comes to those who live close to God through prayer and who want what He wants. That keeps their lives from shrinking in on themselves until their souls resemble a prune.

I heard of a lady who began investing in the stock market in 1944 and kept doing so until her death at age 101 in 1995. She built a port-folio worth 22 million dollars! But she seems to have lived a loveless, shallow life. Someone who knew her said a big day for her was walking down to her stock broker to visit her stock certificates.

She lived a wasted life because close relation-ships to others and love for God were lacking.

※

We live by faith. As we pray and seek God's will in specific matters, keep in mind that "God has not promised to whisper 'perfect plans' or omniscience into the mind of any believer who asks."[41]

In general, the narrow road may be wider than you think (Matt. 7:14).

※

Many possibilities exist before us. Many choices are equally valid. As mature Christians we are to weigh the choices, apply basic principles for decision-making, and make a mature choice.

> *Whatever your hand finds to do, do it with all your might, for in the grave, where you are going, there is neither working nor planning nor knowledge nor wisdom.*
>
> —ECCLESIASTES 9:10

Thank You, Lord, for the privilege of prayer. Thank You for a mind with which to seek You, a heart with which to love You, and a life with which to serve You.

And Lord, thank You for the journey of learning to pray. I'm still taking baby steps, but take what I've learned and use it for Your glory. In Christ's name, Amen.

Endnotes

1. George Appleton, *Journey for a Soul* (Glasgow: William Collins Sons, 1974), 199–200.

2. *The American Heritage Dictionary of the English Language,* 1969 ed., s.v. "magic."

3. C. S. Lewis, "Does Prayer Really Change Things?" *Faith,* February–March 1989, 8.

4. Dick Rice, quoted by Kenneth L. Woodward, "Why America Prays," *Reader's Digest,* April 1992, 200.

5. Alex Haley, quoted by Walter Anderson, *The Greatest Risk of All* (Boston: Houghton Mifflin, 1988), 240.

6. Donald G. Bloesch, *The Struggle of Prayer* (San Francisco: Harper & Row, 1980), 158.

7. Leon Morris, *The Gospel According to St. Luke,* Tyndale New Testament Commentaries (Grand Rapids: Eerdmans, 1974), 195.

8. Theodore Roosevelt, quoted by Anderson, *The Greatest Risk of All,* 3.

9. Wilf Wilkinson, *Good News in Luke* (Glasgow: William Collins Sons, 1974), 72.

10. G. B. Caird, *Saint Luke,* The Pelican New Testament Commentaries. (Baltimore: Penguin Books, 1963), 152.

11. Herbert Benson, MD, with Marg Stark, *Timeless Healing: The Power and Biology of Belief* (New York: Scribner, 1996), 196.

12. Ibid.

13. Ibid., 300.

14. Blaise Pascal, *Pascal's Pensées*. Translated by W. F. Trotter (New York: E. P. Dutton & Co., Inc., 1958), 277–78

15. Fisher Humphreys, *The Heart of Prayer* (New Orleans: Insight Press, 1980), 89.

16. C. S. Lewis, "Does Prayer Really Change Things?" *Faith,* February–March 1989, 9.

17. Blaise Pascal, *Pensees,* 513.

18. Robert H. Mounce, *Matthew: A Good News Commentary* (San Francisco: Harper & Row, 1985), 54.

19. Samuel Johnson, quoted by Og Mandino, *Secrets for Success and Happiness* (New York: Fawcett Columbine, 1995), 240.

20. Humphreys, *The Heart of Prayer,* 55–56.

21. Ibid., 57–58.

22. Lewis Grizzard, "A Miracle of Recovery Called Prayer," 13 May 1993, from his syndicated newspaper column.

23. Blaise Pascal, quoted by Mandino, *Secrets for Success and Happiness,* 200.

24. Henry D. Thoreau, quoted by Mandino, "Preface," in *Secrets for Success and Happiness.*

25. Charles H. Rabon, "Be Still and Know: An Experiment in Prayer," *Quarterly Review,* January–March 1988, 35.

26. This letter is from Bruce Larsen, *Dare to Live Now* (Grand Rapids: Zondervan, 1965), 83.

27. C. S. Lewis, "Does Prayer Really Change Things?" in *Faith,* February–March 1989, 8.

28. Curtis C. Mitchell, "Why Keep Bothering God?" *Christianity Today,* 13 December 1985, 34.

29. P. T. Forsyth, quoted by Mitchell, "Why Keep Bothering God?" 34.

30. These findings are from Dr. Herbert Benson, *The Relaxation Response* (New York: Morrow, 1975), and are well summarized by Dr. Kenneth Cooper in *It's Better to Believe* (Nashville: Nelson, 1995), 28. For further reading see another of Benson's books, *Timeless Healing: The Power of Biology and Belief,* with Marg Stark (New York: Scribner, 1996).

31. Cooper, *It's Better to Believe,* 28.

32. Gary Friesen, with J. Robin Maxson, *Decision Making and the Will of God: A Biblical Alternative to the Traditional Approach* (Portland: Multnomah, 1980), 182. Italics mine.

33. Ibid., 86.

34. Ibid., 113.

35. For further discussion on this, see Humphreys, *The Heart of Prayer,* 54–55.

36. Packer, quoted by Friesen, with Maxson, *Decision Making and the Will of God,* 188.

37. Friesen, with Maxson, *Decision Making and the Will of God,* 193.

38. Friesen, with Maxson, *Decision Making and the Will of God,* 245.

39. Humphreys, *The Heart of Prayer,* 92.

40. Ibid., 93.

41. Friesen, with Maxson, *Decision Making and the Will of God,* 261.

Notes

Notes

Notes

Notes

Notes

Notes

Notes